THE EUROPEAN UNION

Jilly Hunt

raintree 🍃

a Capstone company — publishers for children

Raintree is an imprint of Capstone Global Library Limited, a company incorporated in England and Wales having its registered office at 264 Banbury Road, Oxford, OX2 7DY – Registered company number: 6695582

www.raintree.co.uk
myorders@raintree.co.uk

Edited by Helen Cox Cannons
Designed by Sarah Bennett
Original illustrations © Capstone Global Library Limited 2018
Picture research by Tracy Cummins
Production by Kathy McColley
Originated by Capstone Global Library Limited
Printed and bound in India

ISBN 978 1 4747 6239 7
22 21 20 19 18
10 9 8 7 6 5 4 3 2 1

British Library Cataloguing in Publication Data
A full catalogue record for this book is available from the British Library.

Acknowledgements
We would like to thank the following for permission to reproduce images: Alamy: KEYSTONE Pictures USA, 6; Getty Images: Carol Guzy/The Washington Post, 9; Shutterstock: ahau1969, 16 BL, Anastasios71, 17 Middle, Andrew Mayovskyy, 19 MR, Andrey Shcherbukhin, 18 TM, anitasstudio, 17 BR, Claudio Divizia, 24, dimbar76, 18 MR, dimitris_k, 22, Dreamer4787, 19 BR, DutchScenery, Back Cover, 1, Elena Rostunova, 27, emperorcosar, 19 MB, Fedor Selivanov, 17 TL, Flas100, Design Element, Frederic Legrand - COMEO, 26, Gorodenkoff, 15, Hadrian, Cover, H-a-pp-y, Design Element, Ikars, 20, 21, KadriHarm, 18 TL, kirill_makarov, 18 TR, lensfield, 17 BL, Leonid Andronov, 17 TM, MarinaDa, 16 TM, mije_shots, 10, mkos83, 11, MNStudio, 19 TL, Ms Jane Campbell, 25, Nataliya Nazarova, 16 TL, 19 BL, Nattee Chalermtiragool, 16 BR, Nikolay Antonov, 18 BL, Peter Braakmann, 14, Peteri, 8, photo.ua, 16 TR, pupsy, Design Element, RastoS, 19 ML, Roman Babakin, 19 TR, RossHelen, 18 MB, S.Borisov, 17 TR, Serban Bogdan, 13, S-F, 16 MB, stdesign, 18 ML, Steve Allen, Design Element, Strejman, 5, 28 Left, Sunflowerr, 7, TatjanaRittner, Design Element, Tetiana Yurchenko, 28-29, tetiana_u, 18 BR, TissaNsk, Design Element, Tolga Sezgin, 12, VictoriaSh, 17 MB, Yuriy Vlasenko, 4 BR; SuperStock: André Gonçalves/age fotostock, 23.

We would like to thank Professor Simon Bulmer, FAcSS from the Department of European Politics at the University of Sheffield for his invaluable help in the preparation of this book.

Contents

Some words in this book appear in bold, **like this**.
You can find out what they mean by looking in the glossary.

What is the European Union?

The European Union, or the EU for short, is a group of countries that have agreed to work together. The EU aims to improve everyone's lives by working together to make each EU country stronger. They aim to encourage every country to:

- improve economically – to make more money
- improve socially – for example, ensuring every child receives an education
- protect people's human rights – for instance, putting limits on the number of hours people have to work
- protect the environment.

The EU also agrees laws that help protect people and the environment and aim to make lives better. For example, there are laws that try to protect us against air, noise and water pollution.

The circle of gold stars on the EU flag stands for the ideals of unity and harmony in Europe. ▲

The "four freedoms"

Countries that are part of the EU have the benefit of the "four freedoms". These are the freedom of movement of **goods**, **services**, people and money. EU **citizens** can travel freely within the EU and live, work or study in whichever country they choose. In a similar way, EU businesses can sell their goods or services in any EU country. If they were not part of the EU they would have to pay **taxes** (an extra charge) to be able to sell their goods or services in another country.

EuroFact!

In 2017, the EU had a population of over 508 million people. This is the world's third-biggest population after those of China and India.

▲ World map showing the countries of the EU.
Turn to pages 28–29 for a bigger map of the EU.

The history of the EU

The first step to creating a union of European countries came after the hardships and tragedies of World War II (1939–1945). Leaders in six countries had the idea to work together to control the production of coal and steel. These materials were vital to rebuilding homes, buildings and roads destroyed in the war. They are also key materials for making weapons. By deciding together what to do with their coal and steel, no one country could secretly make weapons. The group also believed they would not want to go to war against each other because they would rely on each other too much. So, in 1951, Belgium, France, Germany, Italy, Luxembourg and the Netherlands formed the European Coal and Steel Community (ECSC).

▲ Robert Schuman (right) was an important person in bringing European countries together.

EuroFact!

Europe Day is held on 9 May. It marks the anniversary of a speech made in 1950 by the French Foreign Minister, Robert Schuman. He called for European countries to work together to prevent future wars and bring peace to Europe.

The European Economic Community

The ECSC showed the benefits of working together. In 1958, the same six countries set up the European Economic Community (EEC) to cover all industries. Until then, **quotas** restricted the amount of goods one country could sell within another country. The EEC removed these barriers and made it easier for countries to **trade** with each other. The EEC also put in place a single way of trading with non-member countries and made it easier to transport goods between countries. It helped workers to move between member countries, too.

Countries of the European Union

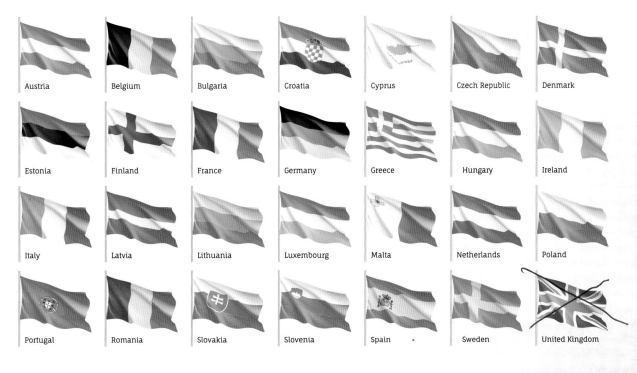

Austria	Belgium	Bulgaria	Croatia	Cyprus	Czech Republic	Denmark
Estonia	Finland	France	Germany	Greece	Hungary	Ireland
Italy	Latvia	Lithuania	Luxembourg	Malta	Netherlands	Poland
Portugal	Romania	Slovakia	Slovenia	Spain	Sweden	United Kingdom

▲ From the first agreement between just 6 countries, the EU grew to include 28 countries in 2018.

The European Communities

In 1967, the ECSC and EEC merged with the European Atomic Energy Community (Euratom) to become the European Communities (EC). This community grew in 1973 when Denmark, the UK and Ireland joined. It grew again in 1981, when Greece joined the community. In 1986, Portugal and Spain joined, bringing the total to 12 countries.

The European Union

The European Union was officially founded on 1 November 1993. This new union brought the twelve EC countries closer together politically and financially.

A changing Europe

In the late 1980s and early 1990s, momentous political events happened that changed Europe. The collapse of **Communism** led to the break-up of the **Soviet Union** and civil wars caused the division of Communist **Yugoslavia**. This resulted in more countries wanting to be part of the European community. Countries wanted to take advantage of the benefits of EU membership to help them improve.

▶ This map shows the countries in Europe that had Communist rule.

countries under Communist rule

Need to know

Communism is a system of government in which there is no private ownership. Instead, everything belongs to the community or the state. The Communist theory is that the government divides out wealth according to individual need. But the reality for those living in Eastern Europe and the Soviet Union was poverty and starvation for millions.

The Soviet Union was ruled by a series of dictators, most notably Joseph Stalin. Stalin used terror and fear to control people from about 1929 until his death in 1953. In 1985, Mikhail Gorbachev became the leader of the Communist Party in the Soviet Union. He allowed some democratic elections. Other Eastern European countries followed, and the system of Communism finally collapsed in 1989–90.

▼ In 1989, East Germany's Communist government fell. The wall that divided East and West Germany was broken down and Germany became one country again.

Why do countries want to join the EU?

Countries of the world trade the goods they produce with other countries. Some countries have special trade deals. This makes it harder or more expensive for other countries to sell or buy goods. Countries may also impose higher taxes on goods that come from other lands. Taxes are a part of the price of the goods or services that goes to the government of that country. Some countries also have quotas in place. These quotas limit how much of a particular product can be bought or sold. Countries within the EU can trade with each other without any of these barriers.

▼ This container ship in the German port of Hamburg is loaded with goods that may be heading for sale throughout Europe or the rest of the world.

The single market

One of the main reasons countries want to be part of the EU is because of the single market. A market is a place where business can be done – where goods can be bought and sold, or services offered and paid for. A single market is formed when a number of countries agree that business can be done without any **restrictions**. Goods and money can be moved freely across countries' borders. Having no restrictions means that companies can earn more money, so countries and people become wealthier.

▼ The euro currency was introduced in 2002.

EuroFact!

As well as a single market, some countries wanted a single currency. In 2002, the euro was introduced in 11 EU countries – Austria, Belgium, Finland, France, Germany, Ireland, Italy, Luxembourg, the Netherlands, Portugal and Spain. The euro replaced their own currencies. By 2017, 19 EU countries used the euro. They are said to be part of the "Eurozone".

What are the rules for joining the EU?

The European Union is like a club and if a country wants to be a member it has to pay a membership fee and agree to keep to the club's rules. In return, the country receives certain benefits.

To be a member of the EU, a country must:

- have a democratic government. This means the government must allow the citizens the right to vote for the people they want to run their country
- follow EU laws with the right to a fair trial and justice for all

▲ As of 2018, it was not certain that Turkey would join the EU. Both sides had doubts about each other, and there had been protests against Turkey's membership.

EuroFact!

Countries that in 2018 were working to adopt EU laws so they could join the European Union:
- Albania
- Montenegro
- Serbia
- The Former Yugoslav Republic of Macedonia
- Turkey

▲ This map shows the location of The Former Yugoslav Republic of Macedonia and the area within Greece known as Macedonia.

- protect all people, including **minority groups**. Everyone must be treated equally, with respect and have freedoms such as the right to an education

- be able to cope economically with competition and market forces in the EU. The EU expects a country's economy to be free from state control. Businesses should be able to make their own decisions.

▲ The aim of the EU is to help improve lives by working together. These local children in the Netherlands are welcoming refugee children into their community.

Paying into the EU

As part of its membership, each country pays money into the EU. There is no fixed amount. Instead, countries pay about 1 per cent of what they earn in the year. Their earnings are called their **Gross National Income**. This system is supposed to make it fair for every country to try to improve the lives of all Europeans. However, some people feel that it is not fair for the wealthier countries to be paying more money than the poorer countries. For example, in 2015 the UK contributed €18.209 billion and Germany contributed €24.283 billion to the EU. In the same year, Romania contributed €1.319 billion and Lithuania contributed €0.316 billion.

What is the money used for?

EU money is used to help each country encourage growth in its economy and employment. It is also used to support **rural** development and agriculture. For example, British farmers received funding for using farming techniques that help the environment.

EuroFact!

EU money helps to fund projects that will help everyone. For example, an EU-funded research team is working on ways of making cancer drugs more effective. Another team is finding new solutions to make rivers and lakes cleaner, safer and more sustainable.

The money paid into the EU helps to fund projects in all EU countries, such as protecting the environment. EU money is also used to help with global issues such as trying to reduce poverty in poorer countries outside of the EU.

Countries of the EU

Belgium

Size (km²): 30,528
Population size (2016): 11,311,117
Official EU language(s): Dutch, French
    and German
Capital city: Brussels
Currency: Euro €
€ paid into EU (2015): 3.692 billion
€ received in funding (2015): 6.952 billion

EU member since 1 January 1958

France

Size (km²): 633,287
Population size (2016): 66,759,950
Official EU language(s): French
Capital city: Paris
Currency: Euro €
€ paid into EU (2015): 19.013 billion
EU spending in € (2015): 14.468 billion

EU member since 1 January 1958

Germany

Size (km²): 357,376
Population size (2016): 82,175,684
Official language: German
Capital city: Berlin
Currency: Euro €
€ paid into EU (2015): 24.283 billion
EU spending in € (2015): 11.013 billion

EU member since 1 January 1958

Italy

Size (km²): 302,073
Population size (2016): 60,665,551
Official language: Italian
Capital city: Rome
Currency: Euro €
€ paid into EU (2015): 14.232 billion
EU spending in € (2015): 12.338 billion

EU member since 1 January 1958

Luxembourg

Size (km²): 2,586
Population size (2016): 576,249
Official languages: French, German
Capital city: Luxembourg
Currency: Euro €
€ paid into EU (2015): 0.350 billion
EU spending in € (2015): 1.649 billion

EU member since 1 January 1958

Netherlands

Size (km²): 41,542
Population size (2016): 16,979,120
Official language: Dutch
Capital city: Amsterdam
Currency: Euro €
€ paid into EU (2015): 5.759 billion
EU spending in € (2015): 2.359 billion

EU member since 1 January 1958

Ireland

Size (km²): 69,797
Population size (2016): 4,724,720
Official languages: Irish, English
Capital city: Dublin
Currency: Euro €
€ paid into EU (2015): 1.558 billion
EU spending in € (2015): 2.009 billion

EU member since 1 January 1973

UK

Size (km²): 248,528
Population size (2016): 65,382,556
Official language: English
Capital city: London
Currency: Pound sterling £
€ paid into EU (2015): 18.209 billion
EU spending in € (2015): 7.458 billion

EU member since 1 January 1973
(Due to leave in 2019)

Denmark

Size (km²): 42,924
Population size (2016): 5,707,251
Official language: Danish
Capital city: Copenhagen
Currency: Danish krone DKK
€ paid into EU (2015): 2.191 billion
EU spending in € (2015): 1.529 billion

EU member since 1 January 1973

Greece

Size (km²): 131,957
Population size (2016): 10,783,748
Official language: Greek
Capital city: Athens
Currency: Euro €
€ paid into EU (2015): 1.206 billion
EU spending in € (2015): 6.210 billion

EU member since 1 January 1981

Austria

Size (km²): 83,879
Population size (2016): 8,690,076
Official language: German
Capital city: Vienna
Currency: Euro €
€ paid into EU (2015): 2.529 billion
EU spending in € (2015): 1.787 billion

EU member since 1 January 1995

Portugal

Size (km²): 92,226
Population size (2016): 10,341,330
Official language: Portuguese
Capital city: Lisbon
Currency: Euro €
€ paid into EU (2015): 1.529 billion
EU spending in € (2015): 2.595 billion

EU member since 1 January 1986

Spain

Size (km²): 505,944
Population size (2016): 46,445,828
Official language: Spanish
Capital city: Madrid
Currency: Euro €
€ paid into EU (2015): 8.772 billion
EU spending in € (2015): 13.696 billion

EU member since 1 January 1986

Finland

Size (km²): 338,440
Population size (2016): 5,487,308
Official language: Finnish, Swedish
Capital city: Helsinki
Currency: Euro €
€ paid into EU (2015): 1.729 billion
EU spending in € (2015): 1.330 billion

EU member since 1 January 1995

Sweden

Size (km²): 438,574
Population size (2016): 9,851,017
Official language: Swedish
Capital city: Stockholm
Currency: Swedish krona SEK
€ paid into EU (2015): 3.513 billion
EU spending in € (2015): 1.468 billion

EU member since 1 January 1995

Cyprus

Size (km²): 9,251
Population size (2016): 848,319
Official language: Greek
Capital city: Nicosia
Currency: Euro €
€ paid into EU (2015): 0.212 billion
EU spending in € (2015): 0.203 billion

EU member since 1 May 2004

Czech Republic

Size (km²): 78,868
Population size (2016): 10,553,843
Official language: Czech
Capital city: Prague
Currency: Czech koruna CZK
€ paid into EU (2015): 1.315 billion
EU spending in € (2015): 7.075 billion

EU member since 1 May 2004

Estonia

Size (km²): 45,227
Population size (2016): 1,315,944
Official language: Estonian
Capital city: Tallinn
Currency: Euro €
€ paid into EU (2015): 0.185 billion
EU spending in € (2015): 0.443 billion

EU member since 1 May 2004

Hungary

Size (km²): 93,011
Population size (2016): 9,830,485
Official language: Hungarian
Capital city: Budapest
Currency: Hungarian Forint HUF
€ paid into EU (2015): 0.946 billion
EU spending in € (2015): 5.629 billion

EU member since 1 May 2004

Latvia

Size (km²): 64,573
Population size (2016): 1,968,957
Official language: Latvian
Capital city: Riga
Currency: Euro €
€ paid into EU (2015): 0.206 billion
EU spending in € (2015): 0.982 billion

EU member since 1 May 2004

Malta

Size (km²): 315
Population size (2016): 434,403
Official languages: Maltese, English
Capital city: Valletta
Currency: Euro €
€ paid into EU (2015): 0.092 billion
EU spending in € (2015): 0.134 billion

EU member since 1 May 2004

Lithuania

Size (km²): 65,286
Population size (2016): 2,888,558
Official language: Lithuanian
Capital city: Vilnius
Currency: Euro €
€ paid into EU (2015): 0.316 billion
EU spending in € (2015): 0.877 billion

EU member since 1 May 2004

Poland

Size (km²): 312,679
Population size (2016): 37,967,209
Official language: Polish
Capital city: Warsaw
Currency: Polish Zloty PLN
€ paid into EU (2015): 3.718 billion
EU spending in € (2015): 13.358 billion

EU member since 1 May 2004

Slovenia

Size (km²): 20,273
Population size (2016): 2,064188
Official language: Slovenian
Capital city: Ljubljana
Currency: Euro €
€ paid into EU (2015): 0.341 billion
EU spending in € (2015): 0.940 billion

EU member since 1 May 2004

Slovakia

Size (km²): 49,035
Population size (2016): 5,426,252
Official language: Slovak
Capital city: Bratislava
Currency: Euro €
€ paid into EU (2015): 0.608 billion
EU spending in € (2015): 3.735 billion

EU member since 1 May 2004

Bulgaria

Size (km²): 110,370
Population size (2016): 7,153,784
Official language: Bulgarian
Capital city: Sofia
Currency: Bulgarian lev BGN
€ paid into EU (2015): 0.424 billion
EU spending in € (2015): 2.730 billion

EU member since 1 January 2007

Romania

Size (km²): 238,391
Population size (2016): 19,760,314
Official language: Romanian
Capital city: Bucharest
Currency: Romanian Leu
€ paid into EU (2015): 1.319 billion
EU spending in € (2015): 6.538 billion

EU member since 1 January 2007

Croatia

Size (km²): 56,594
Population size (2016): 4,190,669
Official language: Croatian
Capital city: Zagreb
Currency: Croatian Kuna HRK
€ paid into EU (2015): 0.357 billion
EU spending in € (2015): 0.605 billion

EU member since 1 July 2013

How is the EU run?

The EU is run by different groups of people with different responsibilities. Understanding how the EU works can be confusing because some of the names of the organizations are quite similar. The Council of the European Union is different from the European Council, for example!

Together, the different EU groups work to improve lives of EU citizens by putting in place rules about most areas of life. There are EU rules about the quality of drinking water and the ingredients that go into food. EU agreements even mean that major events, such as the Olympics or the football World Cup, are shown on regular TV, rather than pay-TV channels.

▲ The main offices of the European Parliament are in Brussels, Belgium.

EU institutions and bodies

EU Parliament

- 751 members are voted for by citizens of each EU country
- Makes EU laws
- Supervises other EU groups
- Sets and approves EU budgets

European Council

- Made up of the leaders of the EU countries, the European Commission President and the High Representative for Foreign Affairs and Security Policy
- Meets about every three months to discuss current issues and decide on the priorities of the EU
- Decisions are mostly taken by consensus – getting everyone to agree

European Commission

- Proposes new EU laws and rules to help EU citizens
- Puts into place actions agreed upon by the European Parliament and the Council of the EU
- Responsible for spending the EU budget

Council of the EU

- Made up of government ministers from each EU country
- Together with the European Parliament, makes EU laws and sets the yearly EU budget
- Works on the EU's foreign and security policy to try to keep EU citizens safe

High Representative for Foreign Affairs and Security Policy/Vice President of the Commission

- Stands for the EU at international meetings

European Court of Justice

- Makes sure EU law is followed

European Central Bank

- Looks after EU money

European Court of Auditors

- Makes sure EU funds are collected and used correctly

What happens when things go wrong?

One of the biggest challenges to be faced by the EU was caused by a **global recession**. The downturn in economies around the world in 2009 led to a debt crisis in some EU countries. These countries found themselves owing large amounts of money that they couldn't pay back.

Need to know

A debt is when someone owes money to someone else. Governments are often in debt, which has usually built up over a number of years. They borrow money to pay back what they owe. But they also borrow money to invest in projects that they hope will make the country richer in the future.

▼ People queued to take out money during the economic crisis in Greece. They no longer trusted the banks.

The Eurozone crisis

The debt crisis started in Greece but Portugal, Ireland, Cyprus and Spain soon had their own economic problems.

These countries are part of the Eurozone and so they use the euro as their currency. Because it is a shared currency, what happens in one country affects other Eurozone countries. For differing reasons, the crisis led to the governments of Greece, Portugal, Ireland, Cyprus and Spain needing financial support. This worried the EU because it put the value of the euro at risk. So the EU loaned billions of dollars to these countries' governments. In return, these governments had to promise to reduce the amount they were spending.

As part of the deal, these governments were forced to cut services and increase taxes. This made life harder for people living in these countries. People lost their jobs and did not have enough money to live on. Hundreds and thousands held protests to show their governments their feelings.

▲ Huge crowds protest against tax rises in Portugal as the government tries to cut its costs.

Brexit and "Euroscepticism"

One of the main challenges that the EU faces is the growth of "Euroscepticism". A Eurosceptic is someone who wants to limit links to the EU or wants no ties at all. Countries such as the UK and France have seen an increase in the number of people supporting Eurosceptic political parties. Many Eurosceptics are unhappy with the economic conditions in Europe. They want more powers returned to their country's national government instead of feeling controlled by the EU.

Brexit

In February 2016, the then British Prime Minister, David Cameron, announced that a **referendum** would be held in June of the same year. The referendum gave the British people a chance to vote on whether the UK should stay or leave the EU. This vote was nicknamed "Brexit", which is short for "British exit".

▶ The voting slip for the 2016 referendum had just one question for voters to answer.

Referendum on the United Kingdom's membership of the European Union

Vote only once by putting a cross ☒ in the box next to your choice

Should the United Kingdom remain a member of the European Union or leave the European Union?

Remain a member of the European Union

Leave the European Union

Referendum results

The result was very close. Overall, 48 per cent of British voters wanted to stay within the EU, but nearly 52 per cent voted to leave. In Scotland and Northern Ireland, most people voted to remain. Yet the overall UK result was used to make the decision.

Brexit results per country

COUNTRY	LEAVE	REMAIN
England	53.4%	46.6%
Northern Ireland	44.2%	55.8%
Scotland	38.0%	62.0%
Wales	52.5%	47.5%
UK total	51.9%	48.1%

▼ People who were unhappy with the 2016 referendum result held protest marches to let the British government know about their feelings.

What happens next?

The UK government began the process of leaving the EU after the referendum. The first step was for Britain to "trigger Article 50". Article 50 is the section of an EU agreement about what happens if a member country wants to leave. Britain had to tell the EU that it wanted to leave and then start doing the things listed in Article 50.

Need to know

The British Prime Minister, Theresa May, needed the permission of Parliament before she was allowed to trigger Article 50. It was triggered on 29 March 2017.

Leaving the EU

The UK then had two years to leave the EU. However, no country has ever left the EU before and some experts think that it will take longer.

The process of leaving the EU is complicated because there are lots of ways the EU impacts on the UK. For example, current EU laws need to be adopted into British law so that there is no gap in the rules once Britain leaves. Once the UK is independent from the EU, it will be able to decide its own laws and make its own trade deals.

How will Brexit affect me?

We can't say for sure how Brexit will affect the UK because the changes will take many years. You can keep up to date with these changes by watching news programmes such as CBBC's *Newsround* or reading newspapers such as *First News*.

▲ In 2016, about 3.6 million people from other EU countries were living in the UK. In 2015, about 1.2 million British people lived in other EU countries.

Map of the European Union

This map shows the location of the EU countries.
When Britain triggered Article 50, it agreed to leave the EU by 29 March 2019.

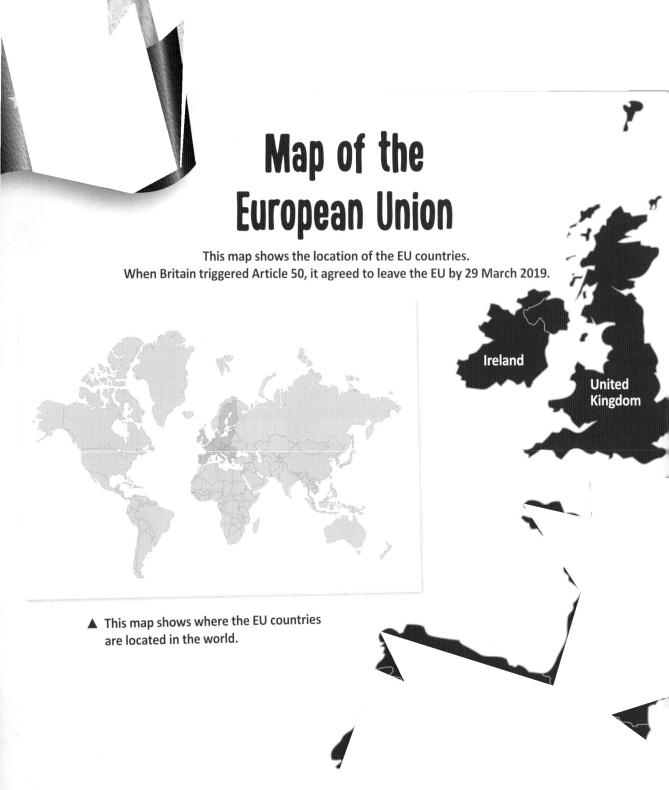

Ireland

United Kingdom

▲ This map shows where the EU countries are located in the world.

Estonia

Latvia

Lithuania

Denmark

Netherlands

Germany

Belgium

Luxembourg

Poland

Czech Republic

Slovakia

Austria

Hungary

Slovenia

Croatia

Romania

Italy

Bulgaria

Greece

Cyprus

Malta

Glossary

budget amount of money available to spend

citizen person who has the right to belong to a certain country

Communism political system in which the government controls the making of goods and the running of services

currency system of money that a country uses

democratic allowing people to vote for who they want to run the country

dictator ruler who has complete power over a country

Eurozone countries that use the euro as their currency

global recession time when there is less trade and production of goods than usual and many people are out of work all over the world

goods physical items that are bought and sold

Gross National Income total value of goods and services produced by a country and income from abroad

minority group people who have a different culture, religion, language or skin colour from most other people in their society

public consultation discussing a matter with people before deciding what to do

quota limited number of something that is allowed

referendum opportunity for people to vote to show if they agree with a government policy or not

restriction rule or law that limits what you can do or what can happen

rural to do with the countryside

service activity such as banking or tourism that is part of the economy

Soviet Union (1922–1991) former country ruled from Moscow, in Russia, that had a Communist system of government

sustainable using products and energy in a way that does not harm people or the environment now or in the future

tax sum of money that people or businesses pay to the government to pay for government services

trade buying, selling or exchanging goods or services

Yugoslavia former country made up of the countries now called Serbia, Montenegro, Croatia, Slovenia, Kosovo, Bosnia-Herzegovina and The Former Yugoslav Republic of Macedonia

Find out more

You can get in touch with the European Commission if you want to share your views on EU policies, suggest changes or even suggest new policies. The European Commission allows EU citizens to respond to its **public consultations** on issues: for example, on the trade of ivory within the EU. If you have any questions, you can contact Commission staff in Brussels or your local Commission office.

Keep up to date with Brexit developments by watching or reading the news. Programmes such as CBBC's *Newsround* and newspapers such as *First News* are designed especially for children.

Books

Brexit: Britain's Decision to Leave the European Union, Daniel Nunn (Raintree, 2017)

Democracy (Exploring British Values), Catherine Chambers (Raintree, 2017)

Europe (Mathalon Maps), Joanne Randolph (Raintree, 2016)

Introducing Europe, Anita Ganeri (Raintree, 2013)

What is a Democracy? (Understanding Political Systems), Robyn Hardyman (Raintree, 2017)

What is Communism? (Understanding Political Systems), Karen Latchana Kenney (Raintree, 2017)

Websites

europa.eu/kids-corner/index_en.htm
The EU website for children contains information, games and quizzes. For example, did you know that there are 24 official languages spoken in the EU?

Index